images of banff

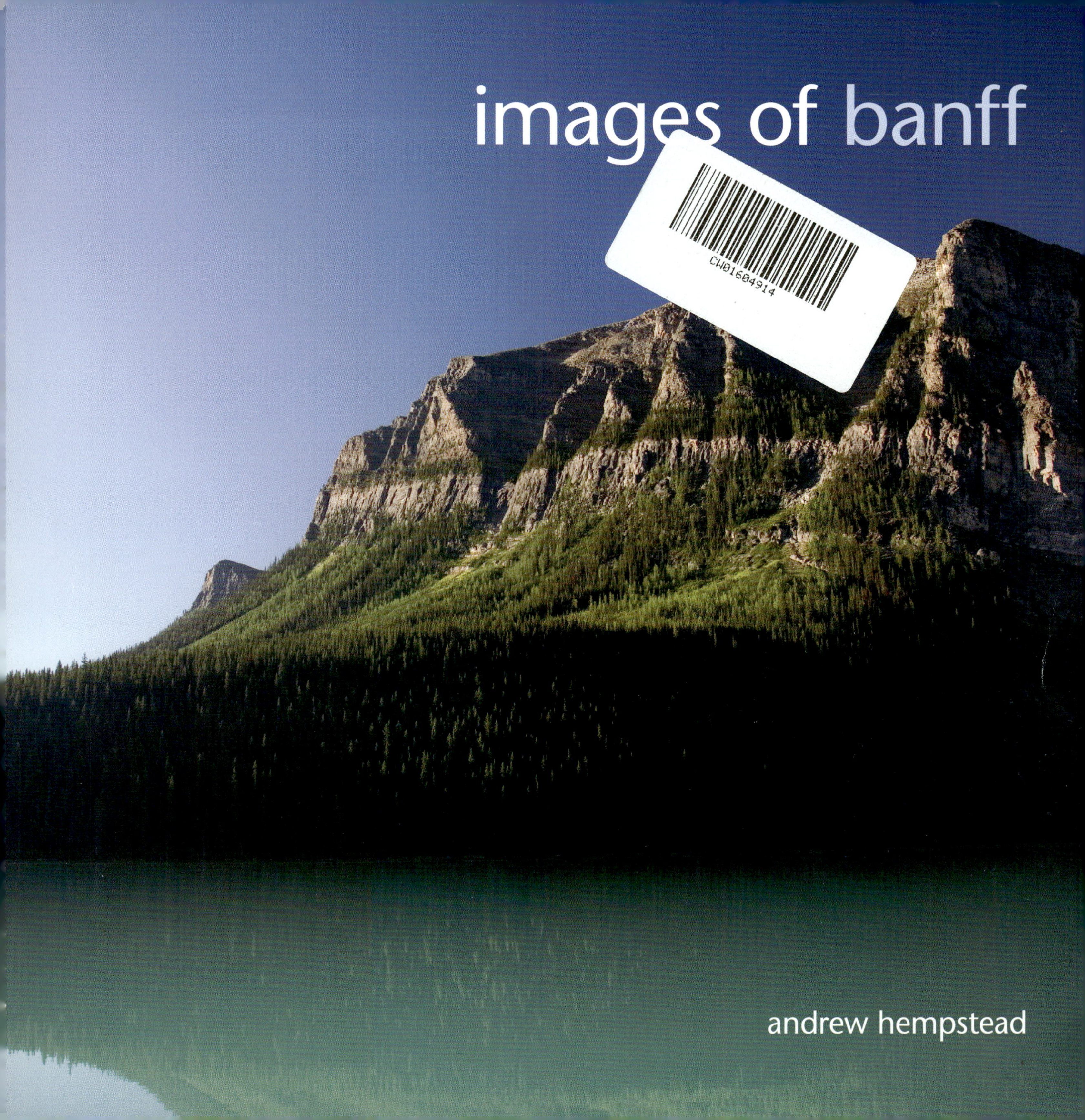

andrew hempstead

RESCUE
40
50
9

Lake Louise (LEFT) *The best way to appreciate the beauty of Lake Louise is from a canoe.*

IMAGES OF BANFF

Published by
Summerthought
Summerthought Publishing
PO Box 2309
Banff, AB T1L 1C1
Canada
www.summerthought.com

Design and production: Linda Petras
Printed and bound in Canada by Friesens

We gratefully acknowledge the financial support of the Alberta Foundation for the Arts for our publishing activities.

Alberta Foundation for the Arts

Library and Archives Canada Cataloguing in Publication

Hempstead, Andrew
Images of Banff / Andrew Hempstead.

ISBN 978-1-926983-08-0
1. Banff National Park (Alta.)—Pictorial works. I. Title.
FC3664.B3H44 201 971.23'32 C2012-901380-3

Herbert Lake, *Icefields Parkway* (FRONT COVER)

Banff Avenue (ABOVE) *Banff Avenue is a major attraction for visitors, especially those who consider shopping and dining an important part of a vacation.*

Peyto Lake (OPPOSITE) *Along the Icefields Parkway, Peyto Lake is notable for its translucent turquoise colouring.*
Indian Paintbrush (RIGHT) *Indian paintbrush brightens the landscape with an intense splash of red.*

introduction

Banff National Park, Canada's oldest and best known national park, encompasses some of the world's most magnificent scenery. Soaring, snowcapped peaks form a spectacular backdrop for glacial lakes, fast-flowing rivers, and endless forests. Deer, moose, elk, mountain goats, bighorn sheep, black and grizzly bears, and wolves inhabit the park's vast wilderness, while the human species is concentrated in the picture-postcard town of Banff and the equally scenic village of Lake Louise—two of North America's most famous resorts. The town of Banff is filled with accommodations to suit all budgets and a wide range of dining and shopping opportunities, while the namesake of the much smaller village of Lake Louise is regarded as one of the seven natural wonders of the world. The lake is rivaled for sheer beauty only by Moraine Lake, just down the road. Just north of Lake Louise, the Icefields Parkway is considered one of the world's most spectacular drives. Its course takes you through a magnificent landscape of lakes, mountains, and waterfalls that will leave you breathless. One of Banff's greatest drawing cards is the accessibility of its natural wonders. Most highlights are close to the road system. But adventurous visitors can follow an excellent system of hiking trails to alpine lakes, along glacial valleys, and to spectacular viewpoints where crowds are scarce and human impact has been minimal. Biking, canoeing, kayaking, white-water rafting, golfing, and fishing are also high in the summertime popularity stakes while in winter visitors don skis, snowboards, and snowshoes.

Downtown skating (OPPOSITE) *Local youngsters take advantage of a crisp winter day to hone their hockey skills.* **Banff Avenue** (RIGHT) *Looking down Banff Avenue toward Cascade Mountain.*

town of banff

Many visitors planning a trip to the Canadian Rockies don't realize that the town of Banff is a bustling commercial centre. The town's location is magnificent. It is spread out along the Bow River, extending to Sulphur Mountain to the south and Tunnel Mountain to the east. In one direction is the towering face of Mount Rundle, and in the other, framed by the buildings along Banff Avenue, is Cascade Mountain. Hotels and motels line the north end of Banff Avenue, while a profusion of shops, boutiques, cafes, and restaurants hugs the south end. At the south end of downtown is the Cave and Basin National Historic Site. Here, in 1883, three young railway workers who were searching for gold on their day off discovered a warm stream flowing out of the lower slopes of Sulphur Mountain. The three men had found not gold, but something just as precious—a hot mineral spring that in time would attract visitors from around the world. After the discovery of the Cave and Basin, many commercial facilities sprang up along what is now Banff Avenue and in 1888 the Banff Springs Hotel, the world's largest hotel at the time, opened above the Bow River. Today, Banff is a bustling town of 8,000 residents that welcomes over three million visitors annually. Those that drag themselves away from the bright lights of Banff Avenue, find a surrounding wilderness laced by hiking trails, scenic drives leading to outstanding viewpoints, and one of the world's best-known golf courses.

Canada Day in Banff (ABOVE) *Nationalistic colours come to the forefront on the first day of every July for a high-spirited parade along Banff Avenue and a packed schedule of events in Central Park.*
Winter sunset (OPPOSITE) *The town of Banff, photographed looking southeast from the lower slopes of Mount Norquay on a cloudless winter evening.*

Mount Norquay (ABOVE) *Locals have been skiing at Mount Norquay since the 1920s.*
Banff Springs Golf Course (OPPOSITE) *Golfers have been enjoying the hallowed fairways of the Banff Springs Golf Course for over 100 years. Pictured is the 4th hole, best known as Devil's Cauldron.*

Banff Park Museum (OPPOSITE) *Opened in 1903, the distinctive Banff Park Museum is a good place to learn about the park's natural's history.*

Cave and Basin National Historic Site (ABOVE) *Banff National Park was established in 1885 to protect hot springs now known as the Cave and Basin.*

Moore Residence (RIGHT) *Although best known for its natural attractions, the streets of Banff are dotted with historic log homes.*

MUSEUM
MUSÉE

Evelyn's Coffee Bar (LEFT) *Popular for its wide range of coffee concoctions, Evelyn's is one of many locally owned businesses along Banff Avenue.*
Western wear (BELOW) *Horses have been an important part of Banff's history—and a cowboy culture still thrives.*
Bow River (RIGHT) *The tranquil beauty of the Bow River is just a short walk from the crowds of Banff Avenue.*

Deer (ABOVE) *Wildlife such as deer (pictured), elk, and bears are often sighted within town limits.*

The Fairmont Banff Springs (OPPOSITE) *One of the world's great mountain resorts, the venerable Banff Springs has been taking in guests since 1888.*

Johnston Canyon (OPPOSITE) *The waterfalls of Johnston Canyon are reached by an easy trail from the Bow Valley Parkway.*
Trembling aspen (RIGHT) *Each September, aspen leaves turn a delightful golden colour.*

around the town of banff

Tantalizingly close to the town of Banff are a number of natural attractions that can be reached by bike or driving. From the town of Banff, a short road leads alongside the shallow Vermilion Lakes, from where there are stunning views back to the distinctive peak of Mount Rundle. This area is an expansive montane wetland that supports a variety of mammals and over 200 species of birds, with some species remaining through winter. One of the most appealing short drives in the vicinity of Banff is along Lake Minnewanka Road, which begins where Banff Avenue ends at the northeast end of town. This paved loop passes Cascade Falls, a popular picnic area at Cascade Ponds, and the remnants of a coalmining town at Bankhead before reaching Lake Minnewanka, the largest body of water in Banff National Park. At the lake, visitors strike out on hiking trails or join a boat cruise up the lake to Devil's Gap. The remaining section of the loop passes a viewpoint over Two Jack Lake, and offers the park's most reliable spot for viewing bighorn sheep. Between Banff and Lake Louise, the Bow Valley Parkway is a scenic alternative to the Trans-Canada Highway. Along this route are several impressive viewpoints, interpretive displays, picnic areas, good hiking, and great opportunities for viewing wildlife such as elk and bears. Highlights include the easy walking trail up Johnston Canyon to two impressive waterfalls, the distinctive peak of Castle Mountain, and the many forested picnic areas.

Vermilion Lakes *A short walk from town, the three Vermilion Lakes change dramatically with the season. The lakes come alive with colour each spring* (OPPOSITE), *leaves turn a burnt orange in fall* (RIGHT), *and then in winter the entire area is transformed into a snowy wonderland* (BELOW).

Bighorn sheep (ABOVE) *Easily recognized by curled horns, bighorn sheep are common along Lake Minnewanka Road.*
Two Jack Lake (OPPOSITE) *On a calm morning, the view of Mount Rundle reflected in Two Jack Lake is one of utter tranquility.*

Lake Louise (OPPOSITE) *It is claimed that Lake Louise is one of the world's most photographed lakes.*
Welcome to Lake Louise (RIGHT) *This colourful sign welcomes visitors to Lake Louise.*

lake louise

The jewel-like waters of Lake Louise are a major contributor to Banff National Park being one of Canada's most beautiful destinations. Less than an hour's drive from the town of Banff, the lake has come to symbolize the beauty of the Canadian Rockies—no small feat in a region overrun with natural attractions. Add to the palette glacier-clad mountains, subalpine forests, and the intoxicating aroma of blooms beside the Fairmont Chateau Lake Louise and it is impossible not to be awed by the beauty of the lake. A popular walking trail leads along the lake, while others lead to tea houses and lookouts. Nearby is Moraine Lake, which rivals Lake Louise for natural beauty, but is a much quieter destination. In winter, skaters flock to what is sure one of world's most beautiful rinks and skiers and snowboarders heading for the slopes of the Lake Louise ski area. A question often asked by visitors is "Why does Lake Louise have such a stunning turquoise colour?" The answer is "glacial sediment," an obvious sign that Lake Louise—like many other lakes in the Canadian Rockies—is glacially fed. The silt, which has been ground from bedrock by moving ice, is so fine that it does not sink immediately to the bottom of the lake; instead, it is temporarily suspended in the water. Varying concentrations of silt result in variations in colour between lakes and even within one lake, as the rate of changing air temperatures increases and decreases glacial melt through the year.

Lake Louise (RIGHT) *Lake Louise, deemed by many to be one of the world's most beautiful lakes, draws thousands of visitors to Banff National Park.*

Lake Louise Railway Station (ABOVE) *The railway station at Lake Louise has been converted to an upscale restaurant.*
Baker Creek Mountain Resort (ABOVE; RIGHT) *The cabins at Baker Creek Mountain Resort are renowned for their woodsy appeal.*

Lodge of the Ten Peaks (RIGHT) *Impressive log work is the defining feature of the day lodge at the Lake Louise ski area.*

Fairmont Chateau Lake Louise
(OPPOSITE) *Looking down to the Chateau from Fairview Lookout.*

Plain of the Six Glaciers (LEFT) *The Plain of the Six Glaciers trail climbs into a glacially carved valley rimmed by glaciers.*
Lake Agnes Teahouse (BELOW) *Hikers who reach Lake Agnes are rewarded with freshly baked muffins at this historic lakeside teahouse.*

Lake Louise Ice Castle (ABOVE) *A castle carved from blocks of ice is the centrepiece of the skating rink on Lake Louise.*
Skating on Lake Louise (OPPOSITE) *Mother and son playing hockey, seemingly oblivious to the beauty that surrounds them.*

Larch Valley (ABOVE) *In late September, alpine larch needles turn a wonderful golden colour.*
Pika (LEFT) *Listen carefully and you'll hear the shrill whistles of pika in rocky areas around Moraine Lake.*
Moraine Lake (OPPOSITE) *The translucent waters of Moraine Lake perfectly reflect surrounding snowcapped peaks.*

Bow Lake (OPPOSITE) *A picturesque view of Bow Lake from beside the Icefields Parkway.*
Num-Ti-Jah Lodge (RIGHT) *For unequalled historic ambience, make reservations at Num-Ti-Jah Lodge.*

icefields parkway

Snaking through the Canadian Rockies between Lake Louise and Jasper, the 230-kilometer (143-mile) Icefields Parkway is one of the world's most inspiring mountain highways. Leaving the frantic pace of the Trans-Canada Highway behind, the impressive scenery of the Icefields Parkway begins almost immediately. Herbert Lake, usually ice-free by May, is a perfect place for early morning or evening photography, when the Waputik Range and distinctively shaped Mount Temple are reflected in its waters. Next up for northbound travellers is Crowfoot Glacier, a remnant of the last ice age, and then Bow Lake, which fills a deep valley below the impressive peaks of the Continental Divide. Named for legendary guide "Wild" Bill Peyto, it's worth the short walk to a viewpoint overlooking Peyto Lake, a famously scenic body of water surrounded by jagged peaks. The turquoise waters of Lower Waterfowl Lake, the roar of spring runoff passing through Mistaya Canyon, and the forested panorama of the North Saskatchewan River Valley are all worthwhile stops before commencing the long climb up the "Big Bend" to the park's northern boundary and the Columbia Icefield. The scenery alone qualifies the Icefields Parkway as one of the world's great mountain drives, but wildlife-viewing opportunities are an added bonus. Beginning in April, black and grizzly bears begin coming out of hibernation and larger mammals such as bighorn sheep, mountain goats, elk, and moose move to lower elevations in search of snow-free vegetation. Late May, with dandelions blooming along the roadside, is the best time of year for viewing black bears.

Herbert Lake (RIGHT) *Usually ice-free by May, Herbert Lake is an ideal place for early morning or evening photography, when the Waputik Range and distinctively shaped Mount Temple are reflected in its clear waters.*

Lower Waterfowl Lake (ABOVE) *The turquoise colour of Lower Waterfowl Lake is created by suspended glacial silt.*

Black bear (ABOVE) *Black bears are common along the Icefields Parkway, especially in spring.*

Crowfoot Glacier (LEFT) *Clearly visible from the Icefields Parkway, the glacial "claws" have melted in recent decades, but Crowfoot Glacier is an impressive sight nonetheless.*
Ice climbing (BELOW) *The Weeping Wall is a popular destination for experienced ice climbers.*

Peyto Lake (ABOVE) *Named for legendary Banff guide "Wild" Bill Peyto, Peyto Lake is a scenic highlight of the Icefields Parkway.*

Bow Lake (RIGHT) *Enjoy the lake-and-mountain panorama from the shoreline of Bow Lake.*

An elk is silhouetted beside the mountains during a Banff National Park sunrise.